WRITING FOR

Grade 2

Sky Pony Press
New York

Copyright © 2019 by Hollan Publishing, Inc.

Minecraft® is a registered trademark of Notch Development AB.

The Minecraft game is copyright © Mojang AB.

Sky Pony Press books may be purchased in bulk at special discounts for sales promotion, corporate gifts, fund-raising, or educational purposes. Special editions can also be created to specifications. For details, contact the Special Sales Department, Sky Pony Press, 307 West 36th Street, 11th Floor, New York, NY 10018 or info@skyhorsepublishing.com.

Sky Pony® is a registered trademark of Skyhorse Publishing, Inc.®, a Delaware corporation.

Visit our website at www.skyponypress.com.

10 9 8 7 6

Library of Congress Cataloging-in-Publication Data is available on file.

Cover design by Michael Short
Cover illustration by Bill Greenhead
Interior illustrations by Amanda Brack
Book design by Kevin Baier

Print ISBN: 978-1-5107-3767-9

Printed in China

A NOTE TO PARENTS

When you want to reinforce classroom skills at home, it's crucial to have kid-friendly learning materials. This *Writing for Minecrafters* workbook transforms writing practice into an irresistible adventure complete with diamond swords, zombies, skeletons, and creepers. That means less arguing over homework and more fun overall.

Writing for Minecrafters is also fully aligned with National Common Core Standards for 2nd-grade writing. What does that mean, exactly? All of the writing skills taught in this book correspond to what your child is expected to learn in school. This eliminates confusion and builds confidence for greater homework-time success!

Whether it's the joy of seeing their favorite game characters on every page or the thrill of writing about Steve and Alex, there is something in this workbook to entice even the most reluctant writer.

Happy adventuring!

WRITE WHAT YOU KNOW

Look at the characters below. Finish the sentence about each Minecrafting character or mob using what you see or know. The first one is done for you.

1.  Steve is wearing blue pants .

2.  Alex likes _____ .

3.  The Enderman is _____ .

4. A diamond sword is _____ .

5.  A chest is good for _____ .

6.  The Ender dragon can _____ .

7. The Wither has _____ .

8. The Guardian has _____ .

9. 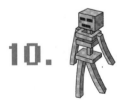 A zombie will _____ .

10. A skeleton is _____ .

CREEPER'S GUIDE TO COLLECTIVE NOUNS

Collective nouns *are words used to describe groups of items. For example, a group of birds is also called a* ***flock*** *of birds.*

Highlight or circle the words below that are collective nouns:

pack	team	army	mushroom
zombie	herd	creeper	stack

Choose three collective nouns above and use them to write sentences about Minecrafting.

1. --

2. --

3. --

A WITCHY DAY

The witch was having a/an _____ day, so she
ADJECTIVE

decided to make a/an _____ potion using
ADJECTIVE

_____ as the main ingredient. She thought it would
NOUN

be funny to throw the potion at a/an _____ ,
ANIMAL

who was in the _____ . It took _____
PLACE IN MINECRAFT   NUMBER

minutes to _____ there. When she opened her
VERB

bag, though, she realized the potion was _____!
ADJECTIVE

The _____ ran off. She gave up and decided
SAME ANIMAL

to go to _____ instead, which was much more
PLACE IN MINECRAFT

_____ .
ADJECTIVE

SENTENCES

A **sentence** is a group of words that tells a complete thought. All sentences begin with a **capital letter**. A statement ends with a **period**. A sentence includes a **noun**, a **verb**, and sometimes an **adjective**.

NOUN
a person, place or thing, like *creeper*

VERB
an action word, like *run*

ADJECTIVE
a describing word, like *scary*

Read the sentences on the opposite page and follow the instructions below.

✦ Draw a triangle around the **capital letter** that begins the sentence.

✦ Circle the **noun** (there may be more than one).

✦ Underline the **verb**.

✦ Draw a rectangle around the **adjective**.

✦ Draw a square around the **period** that ends the sentence.

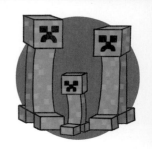

1.   The hungry horse eats a carrot.

2.   The villager trades with a player.

3.    Alex rides a pig.

4.    The nervous creeper explodes.

5.    The skeleton shoots an arrow.

IN THE JUNGLE

Pretend you spawn (start in the game) in the jungle biome. Describe how you would survive. Use details.

If I spawned in the jungle, I would

_____

_____

_____

_____

_____

_____

_____

If I needed food I would . . .

_____

_____

_____

_____

Finally, I would stay safe by . . .

_____

_____

_____

_____

_____

IRREGULAR PAST TENSE VERBS

Fill in the blanks with these irregular past tense verbs.

sat	ran	fought	took	gave

1. The iron golem _____ a flower to the villager.

2. Steve _____ the wither with all his strength.

3. Alex _____ away from an army of skeletons.

4. The chicken _____ on a creeper spawn egg by mistake.

5. The thief _____ everything out of my chest.

WRITE YOUR OPINION

Which of these items is most useful when Minecrafting? Choose one and complete the paragraph below.

A _____ is the most useful item because

_____

_____

_____ .

You can also use this item to _____

_____

_____ .

Finally, it's _____

_____

_____ .

In conclusion, _____ is the most useful item of all the

items above.

WRITING A NARRATIVE

The four pictures below tell a story. Use the pictures to help you tell the story of Alex and Steve trying to get a cow back to its pen. Use the back of the page if needed.

1.

2.

3.

4.

WRITING A NARRATIVE
(continued)

USING DETAILS

Match the sentence to its more detailed version.

1. The Enderman moved toward Steve.

A. The End is a dangerous world where you can battle a dragon.

2. The zombie appeared.

B. Alex uses her pickaxe to mine for lapis lazuli.

3. Alex mines for lapis lazuli.

C. The zombie appeared out of nowhere in gold armor.

4. Diamond swords can destroy things.

D. The tall Enderman teleported toward Steve when Steve made eye contact.

5. The End is dangerous.

E. Diamond swords can destroy blazes, Endermen, and zombies.

ADDING DETAILS

Change the sentences below. Add details to make them more interesting or exciting.

1. I see a villager.

_____

- -

_____

2. The wolf is hungry.

_____

- -

_____

3. I am building a shelter.

_____

- -

_____

4. I have resources.

_____

- -

_____

5. I fight a creeper.

_____

- -

_____

SILLY FILL-IN

Fill in the word blanks below. Read the story on the next page and add your words as you go. Did it make you laugh?

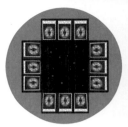

ADJECTIVE a describing word, like *scary*	**NOUN** a person, place or thing, like *creeper*	**VERB** an action word, like *run*

1. _____
   PLACE

2. _____
   VERB

3. _____
   VERB

4. _____
   VERB, PAST TENSE

5. _____
   VERB

6. _____
   VERB

7. _____
   PART OF THE BODY

8. _____
   ADJECTIVE

9. _____
   VERB

10. _____
    ADJECTIVE

11. _____
    NOUN

12. _____
    VERB

13. _____
    NOUN

14. _____
    VERB

15. _____
    ADJECTIVE

16. _____
    SCHOOL SUBJECT

ENDER DRAGON GOES TO THE DENTIST

One day, Steve went to _____ to _____
PLACE   VERB

the Ender dragon. Before he could _____ his
VERB

diamond sword, the Ender dragon stopped him. "I can't fight you

today," he _____ . My tooth is aching so badly, I want
VERB, PAST TENSE

to _____ ." "_____ with me," said Steve,
VERB   VERB

and he took the dragon by the _____ and led him
PART OF THE BODY

through the End portal to a _____village. "This dentist
ADJECTIVE

villager can _____ you and make you feel more
VERB

_____ ," Steve explained. The Ender dragon was
ADJECTIVE

nervous, but he sat in a _____ in the dentist's office and let
NOUN

him _____ the sore tooth. The more nervous the dragon
VERB

became, the more he breathed _____ . Steve used a potion
NOUN

of heat resistance to _____ the dentist, but by the time the
VERB

appointment was over, the dentist was very _____ . When
ADJECTIVE

the dragon left, the dentist breathed a heavy sigh of relief and said, "If

only I had listened to my mother and studied _____ ."
SCHOOL SUBJECT

24

NOUNS IN THE NETHER

Use the **nouns** in the box to complete the sentences about the Nether. Remember, a noun is a person, a place, or a thing.

mushrooms	portal	obsidian	fire	zombie pigman

1. _____ grow all over the ground in the Nether.

2. The Nether is filled with _____ , lava, and dangerous mobs.

3. A _____ is the only way to get to the Nether.

4. You need _____ to build a portal.

5. You can battle a blaze, a ghast, or a _____ in the Nether.

VERBS WITH VILLAGERS

*Use **the verbs** in the box to complete the sentences about villagers. Remember, verbs are action words, like "jump," "make," and "eat."*

plant	trade	run	strikes	become

1. Villagers will _____ you for emeralds.

2. Villagers will _____ away if a zombie attacks.

3. If a zombie attacks a villager, the villager could _____ a zombie villager.

4. A farming villager will _____ and tend crops.

5. If lightning _____ a villager, it turns into a witch.

MINING FOR ADJECTIVES

Use the **adjectives** in the box to complete the sentences about Minecraft. Remember, **adjectives** are describing words, like "funny" and "red."

purple	icy	hostile	poisonous	wooden

1. Polar bears live in _____ biomes.

2. Pufferfish are _____ in the game of Minecraft.

3. A _____ shield will protect you in battle.

4. The shulker hides in its _____ shell.

5. A slime is a _____ mob that hops around.

WRITING IN PAST TENSE

*Use the **past tense** to finish the sentence about how you used to play Minecraft when you were a noob (someone who is new to gaming).*

When I was a noob, I...

1. _____

2. _____

3. _____

4. _____

UNDERWATER FUN

Minecraft is going aquatic! Study the picture for a minute or two. When you think you have memorized the details, try to answer the questions on the back of the page without looking!

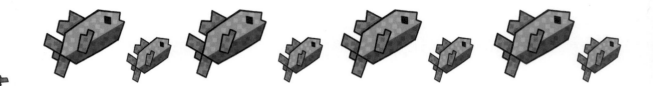

1. How many crabs are in the picture?

_____

- -

_____

2. Name one thing Steve is wearing in the picture.

_____

- -

_____

3. What color is the squid?

_____

- -

_____

4. What underwater predator is swimming at the top of the picture?

_____

- -

_____

5. How many masts are sticking up out of the sunken ship?

_____

- -

_____

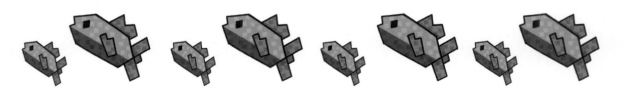

PUNCTUATE IT!

Every sentence should have a capital letter in the beginning and punctuation (like a period) at the end. These sentences are missing both. Write them correctly on the line below.

1. the baby zombie rides a chicken

_____
- -
_____

2. you can tame an ocelot

_____
- -
_____

3. a golden apple can heal you

_____
- -
_____

4. watch out for the zombie pigman

_____
- -
_____

5. don't eat a puffer fish

_____
- -
_____

MIX IT UP!

Put the words in these mixed-up sentences in the correct order. Add a capital letter in the beginning of the sentence and a punctuation mark at the end.

1. amazing Steve an is builder

_____

- -

_____

2. builds Steve bed a

_____

- -

_____

3. is the attacking skeleton

_____

- -

_____

4. bar is hunger my low

_____

- -

_____

5. night come out at zombies

_____

- -

_____

6. spawned desert I in the

_____

- -

_____

7. can spit ghasts fireballs

_____

- -

_____

8. sound creepers make hissing a

_____

- -

_____

9. obsidian is block strong a

_____

- -

_____

10. like ocelots fish eat to

_____

- -

_____

WRITING A NARRATIVE

Someone hid a very valuable object or a secret room behind this Minecraft painting. Write a story where you walk through this mysterious painting. Describe what you discover on the other side and what happens next.

Use the sentence starters below for help:

When I walked through the painting, I saw . . .   Next, I . . .

Suddenly, I . . .   Then I . . .

I couldn't believe . . .   Finally, I . . .

34

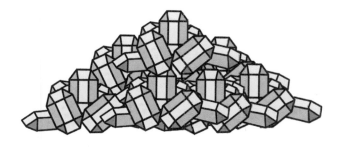

SO MUCH TO DO

Fill in Alex's weekly planner. Use the pictures to help you guess what she wants to do each day. Use a verb (action word) in every entry. Be creative!

MONDAY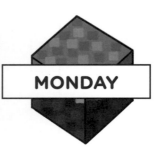

brew some potion

TUESDAY

WEDNESDAY

THURSDAY

FRIDAY

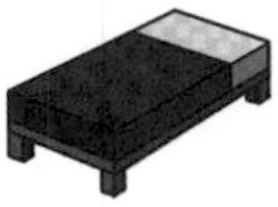

SATURDAY

SUNDAY

SENTENCE GRIEFER

A griefer (a gamer who likes to trick other gamers) wrote these false sentences about Minecrafting. Use the contractions in the word box to make them true. The first one has been done for you. Hint: One contraction is used twice.

don't	aren't	can't	isn't

1. Witches **do** attack villagers.

Witches don't attack villagers.

2. Skeletons **are** peaceful mobs.

_____

_____

3. Zombies **are** safe in the sunlight.

_____

_____

4. Creepers **can** open doors.

_____

_____

5. An enderman **is** an undead mob.

_____

_____

WRITING A TO-DO LIST

Make a Minecrafting TO DO List that includes all the things you want to experience or try in Minecraft.

Things I Want to Do/Learn in Minecraft:

REFLEXIVE PRONOUNS

Rewrite the words in the word box under the correct category: reflexive pronouns or nouns. Hint: Reflexive pronouns are like mirrors: they reflect back to the subject.

~~itself~~	creeper	himself	skeleton	Wither
themselves	ourselves	villager	myself	

REFLEXIVE PRONOUNS

1. itself

2.

3.

4.

5.

NOUNS

1.

2.

3.

4.

HOW TO BUILD A GOLEM

A snow golem is helpful for defending you from hostile mobs. Read the directions for building a Snow Golem. Use the words at the beginning of the sentences to number them in the correct order.

_____ Finally, enjoy watching your snow golem shoot snowballs at your enemies!

_____ Second, stack the two snow blocks on top of each other.

_____ First, make sure you have two snow blocks and a pumpkin in your inventory.

_____ After you stack the snow blocks, place the pumpkin on top of them.

WRITE WHAT YOU KNOW

Look at the Minecrafting pictures below. Finish the sentence about each picture using what you see and know.

1.  Steve is crafting a _____ .

2.  The spider has _____ .

3.  The squid can _____ .

4.  A bow-and-arrow can _____ .

5. Steve holds a _____ .

6. The boat is made of _____ .

7. This chest is _____ .

8. Steve has a _____ .

9. Steve feels _____ .

10. The pig is wearing a _____ .

CREEPER'S COLLECTIVE NOUNS

*Match the **collective noun** to the group it best describes.*

1. trio

2. pack

3. pool

4. cluster

5. hive

6. stack

SILLY FILL-IN

Fill in the word blanks below. Read the story on the next page and add your words as you go. Did it make you laugh?

ADJECTIVE a describing word, like *scary*	**NOUN** a person, place or thing, like *creeper*	**VERB** an action word, like *run*	**ADVERB** a word that describes how you do something, like *slowly*

1. _____
   NOUN

2. _____
   PLURAL NOUN

3. _____
   VERB

4. _____
   PLURAL NOUN

5. _____
   NOUN

6. _____
   PLURAL NOUN

7. _____
   ADVERB

8. _____
   PLURAL NOUN

9. _____
   PLURAL NOUN

10. _____
    ANIMAL

11. _____
    ADJECTIVE

12. _____
    NOUN

13. _____
    ADJECTIVE

14. _____
    VERB

15. _____
    ADJECTIVE

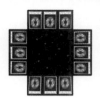

A TRIP TO THE NETHER

Before you enter the Nether, you should know that it's full of

flowing _____ and pools of _____. The
    NOUN   PLURAL NOUN

only reason players dare to _____ here is because it's
             VERB

full of useful _____ like nether _____ and
     PLURAL NOUN   NOUN

blaze _____. Get those items as _____
   PLURAL NOUN   ADVERB

as you can before hostile _____ start to attack. If a
         PLURAL NOUN

ghast starts spitting _____ at you, you might be in big
       PLURAL NOUN

trouble. Watch out for zombie _____ men, too. They are
          ANIMAL

_____ and carry a wooden _____. If you
 ADJECTIVE   NOUN

become surrounded by _____ mobs in the Nether, the
        ADJECTIVE

best thing to do is _____ to the portal and get back to the
       VERB

Overworld before it's too _____.
        ADJECTIVE

IN THE EXTREME HILLS BIOME

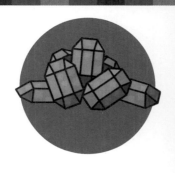

Pretend you spawn (start in the game) in the Extreme Hills Biome. Describe how you would survive. Use details.

If I spawned in the Extreme Hills

Biome, I would...

_____

_____

_____

_____

_____

_____

_____

If I needed food I would...

_____

_____

_____

_____

_____

Finally, I would stay safe by...

_____

_____

_____

_____

_____

_____

SENTENCES

*A **sentence** is a group of words that tells a complete thought. All sentences begin with a **capital letter**. A statement ends with a **period**. A sentence includes a **noun**, a **verb**, and sometimes an **adjective**.*

VERB an action word, like *run*	**ADJECTIVE** a describing word, like *scary*	**NOUN** a person, place or thing, like *creeper*

- Draw a triangle around the **capital letter** that begins the sentence.

- Circle the **noun** (there may be more than one).

- Underline the **verb**.

- Draw a rectangle around the **adjective**.

- Draw a square around the **period** that ends the sentence.

1.  This stew restores my hunger.

2. The skeleton shot me with an arrow.

3. That witch threw a splash potion.

4. An oven cooks raw meat.

5.  An ocelot eats fish.

PLURAL NOUNS

Rewrite the sentences. Change the noun in parentheses to a plural noun and write it on the line. The first one is done for you.

teeth	lives	puppies
witches	people	

1. The (witch) __witches__ live in the swamp biome.

2. Multi-player mode lets you play with other (person) _____.

3. Zombies prefer to live their (life) _____ in the dark.

4. Tame (puppy) _____ will follow their owner around.

5. Creepers do not have any (tooth) _____.

COMPARE AND CONTRAST

Compare these two hostile mobs. How are they the same? Write things that are the same about them in the center of the diagram. Which one is scarier? Bigger? Describe their differences on the sides.

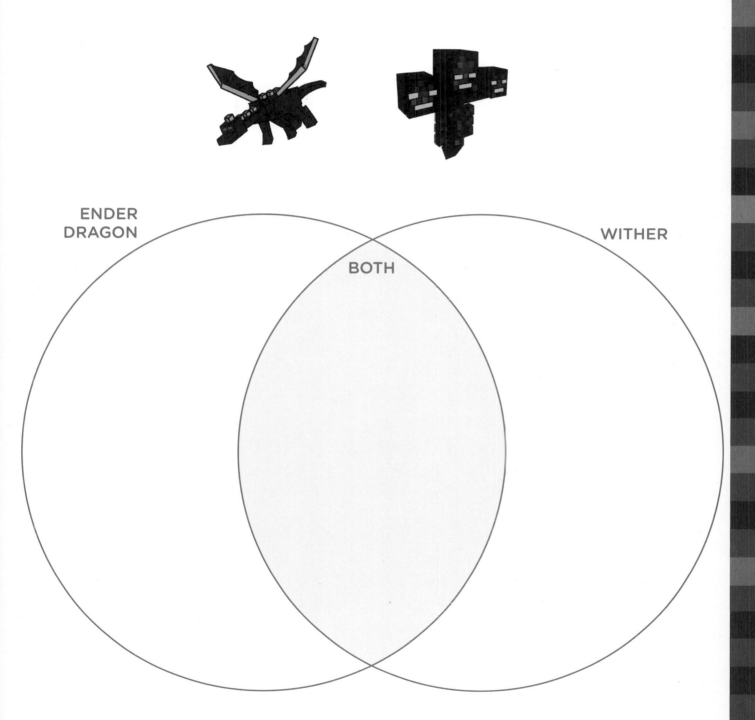

ENDER
DRAGON

BOTH

WITHER

IRREGULAR PAST TENSE VERBS

Fill in the blanks with these irregular past tense verbs.

made	brought	flew	saw	grew

1. Alex _____ her golden sword with her to the End.

2. Steve's flower _____ when he placed bone meal on a grass block.

3. The Ender dragon _____ to an End crystal to regain health.

4. The Enderman _____ me looking at it and teleported over.

5. Steve _____ a fishing rod from three sticks and two pieces of string .

REMEMBERING DETAILS

This gamer's bedroom is very messy! Study the picture for a minute or two. When you think you have memorized the details, try to answer the questions on the back of the page without looking!

REMEMBERING DETAILS

(continued from previous page)

Answer the questions in the space provided.

1. Name one toy on the floor of the bedroom.

_____

- -

_____

2. What object can be seen out the bedroom window?

_____

- -

_____

3. What color is the lamp?

_____

- -

_____

4. What is on top of the bookshelf?

_____

- -

_____

5. What animal shape is hidden in several places?

_____

- -

_____

WRITE YOUR OPINION

Which of these mobs would be most useful to bring to school? Who could you play with at recess? Which one could carry your backpack? Who could get you to and from school the fastest? Choose one and complete the paragraph below.

iron golem

creeper

zombie

Wither

snow golem

The most useful mob to take to school is a _____

_____

because _____

_____

_____

_____

_____

A job this mob could do at my school is _____

_____

_____

In conclusion, a _____

is the most useful mob to bring to school.

CERTIFICATE OF ACHIEVEMENT
CONGRATULATIONS

This certifies that

_____

became a

MINECRAFT WRITING BOSS

on _____.
(date)

_____

Signature

ANSWERS

PAGES 2–3
Write What You Know
Answers may vary, but might include the details below:

2. Alex likes animals.
3. The Enderman is tall.
4. A diamond sword is strong.
5. A chest is good for storing things.
6. The Ender dragon can fly.
7. The Wither has three heads.
8. The Guardian has fins.
9. A zombie will attack.
10. A skeleton is made of bones.

PAGES 4–5
Creeper's Guide to Collective Nouns

pack   team   army   mushroom

zombie   herd   creeper   stack

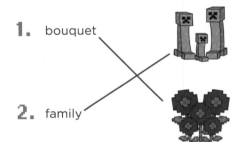

1. bouquet

2. family

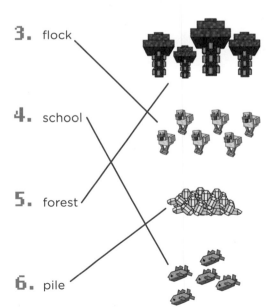

3. flock

4. school

5. forest

6. pile

PAGES 7–8
Silly Fill-In
Answers will vary.

PAGES 8–9
Sentences

1. The hungry horse eats a carrot.
2. The villager trades with a player.
3. Alex rides a pig.
4. The nervous creeper explodes.
5. The skeleton shoots an arrow.

PAGE 10
In the Jungle
Answers will vary.

PAGE 11
Plural Nouns
1. feet
2. wolves
3. Endermen
4. children
5. leaves
6. shelves

PAGES 12–13
Describing in Detail
Answers will vary.

PAGE 14
Compare and Contrast
Answers will vary.

PAGE 15
Irregular Past Tense Verbs

1. gave
2. fought
3. ran
4. sat
5. took

PAGE 16
Write Your Opinion

Answers will vary.

PAGE 17–18
Writing a Narrative

Answers will vary.

PAGE 19
Using Details

1. D
2. C
3. B
4. E
5. A

PAGE 20
Adding Details

Answers will vary, but might include the details below:

1. I see a villager with his arms crossed in a white coat.
2. The white wolf is very hungry because it hasn't eaten in days.
3. I am building a house made of cobblestone and wood.
4. I have helpful resources like food and tools.
5. I fight a green creeper who is about to explode.

PAGE 21
Contractions

1. d
2. f
3. a
4. g
5. b
6. c
7. e

PAGE 22
Contractions

1. Most players **can't** survive a Wither attack.
2. If you are building a house in Minecraft, **don't** forget to add doors to keep out hostile mobs.
3. When **you're** learning to play, set the difficulty to Peaceful or Easy mode.
4. I **wouldn't** get too close to a creeper that's about to explode.

PAGES 23–24
Silly Fill-in

Answers will vary.

PAGE 25
Nouns in the Nether

1. mushrooms
2. fire
3. portal
4. obsidian
5. zombie pigman

PAGE 26
Verbs with Villagers

1. trade
2. run
3. become
4. plant
5. strikes

PAGE 27
Mining for Adjectives
1. icy
2. poisonous
3. wooden
4. purple
5. hostile

PAGE 28
Writing in Past Tense
Answers will vary.

PAGE 29–30
Underwater Fun
1. There is one crab.
2. Steve is wearing goggles. Other answers may include: scuba mask, flippers, and a wetsuit.
3. The squid is black.
4. A shark is swimming at the top of the picture.
5. The sunken ship has two masts.

PAGE 31
Punctuate It!
1. The baby zombie rides a chicken.
2. You can tame an ocelot.
3. A golden apple can heal you.
4. Watch out for the zombie pigman!
5. Don't eat a puffer fish.

PAGE 32
Mix it Up!
1. Steve is an amazing builder.
2. Steve builds a bed.
3. The skeleton is attacking.
4. My hunger bar is low.
5. Zombies come out at night.
6. I spawned in the desert.
7. Ghasts can spit fireballs.
8. Creepers make a hissing sound.
9. Obsidian is a strong block.
10. Ocelots like to eat fish.

PAGE 34–35
Writing a Narrative
Answers will vary.

PAGE 36–37
So Much to Do
Answers will vary, but may include the following:
Tuesday: go fishing
Wednesday: battle a creeper
Thursday: craft a new weapon
Friday: fight the Ender dragon
Saturday: build a bed
Sunday: put valuable items in a chest

PAGE 38
Sentence Griefer
2. Skeletons aren't peaceful mobs.
3. Zombies aren't safe in the sunlight.
4. Creepers can't open doors.
5. An enderman isn't an undead mob.

PAGE 39
Writing a To-Do List
Answers will vary.

PAGE 40
Reflexive Pronouns
Reflexive Pronouns
itself
himself
themselves
ourselves
myself

Nouns
creeper
skeleton
Wither
villager

PAGE 41
How to Build a Golem

___4___ Finally, enjoy watching your snow golem shoot snowballs at your enemies!

___2___ Second, stack the two snow blocks on top of each other.

___1___ First, make sure you have two snow blocks and a pumpkin in your inventory.

___3___ After you stack the snow blocks, place the pumpkin on top of them.

PAGE 42–43
Write What You Know

Answers will vary but may include the following:

1. Steve is crafting a diamond sword.
2. The spider has eight legs.
3. The squid can swim.
4. A bow-and-arrow can be useful.
5. Steve holds a watering can.
6. The boat is made of wood.
7. This chest is open (or empty).
8. Steve has a pencil.
9. Steve feels surprised.
10. The pig is wearing a saddle.

PAGE 44
Creeper's Collective Nouns

1. f
2. c
3. e
4. d
5. b
6. a

PAGE 45–46
Silly Fill-in
Answers will vary.

PAGE 47
In the Extreme Hills Biome
Answers will vary.

PAGE 48–49
Sentences

1. This stew restores my hunger.
2. The skeleton shot me with an arrow.
3. That witch threw a splash potion.
4. An oven cooks raw meat.
5. An ocelot eats fish.

PAGE 50
Plural Nouns

2. people
3. lives
4. puppies
5. teeth

PAGE 51
Compare and Contrast

Answers will vary but may include the following:

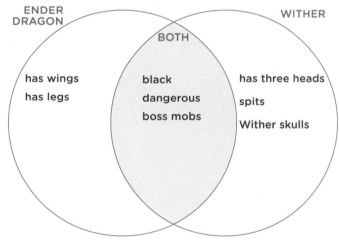

ENDER DRAGON
has wings
has legs

BOTH
black
dangerous
boss mobs

WITHER
has three heads
spits
Wither skulls

PAGE 52
Irregular Past Tense Verbs

1. brought
2. grew
3. flew
4. saw
5. made

PAGE 53–54
Remembering Details

1. There is a soccer ball (as well as a yo-yo, doll, truck, and board game).
2. A tree can be seen through the window.
3. The lamp is purple.
4. There is a plant on top of the bookshelf.
5. A pig shape is hidden in several places.

PAGE 55
Write Your Opinion

Answers will vary.

IF YOU LIKED THIS WORKBOOK, TRY . . .

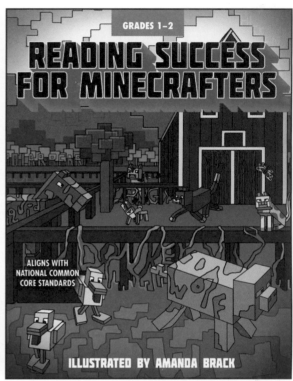

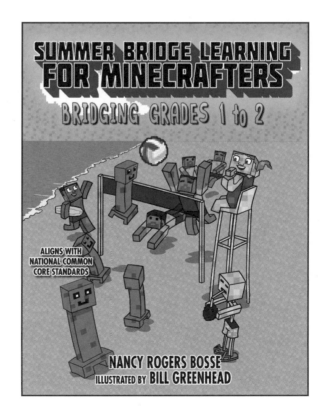